Ode to Wandering

Hope Lukachick

BookLeaf Publishing

Ode to Wandering © 2023 Hope Lukachick

All rights reserved.

Presentation by *BookLeaf Publishing*

Web: www.bookleafpub.com

E-mail: info@bookleafpub.com

ISBN: 9789357740456

First edition 2023

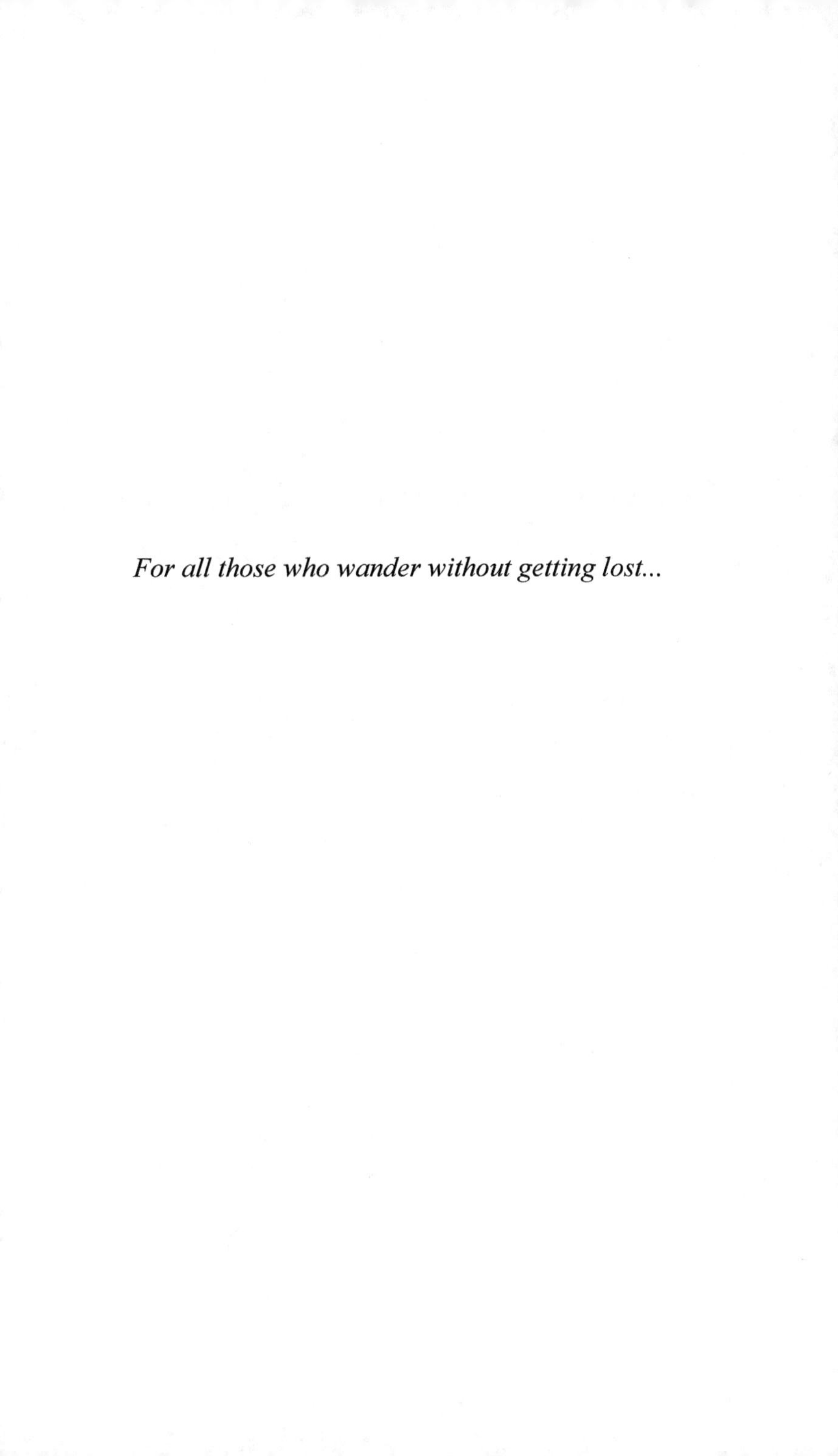

For all those who wander without getting lost...

ACKNOWLEDGEMENT

I want to thank Jesus Christ my savior for giving me the experiences to create the art on these pages. And for all the friends that supported me along my wanderings.

Beginnings

To begin a new era
is to let one end.
To start
is to finish.
To begin
is to end.

How romantically tragic beginnings are.
We must let our constant end,
to begin anew.
To embark on a journey is to
truly call some place home.

Learning to Wander

2

Something's happening to me
I can't quite place it
I feel it tingling beneath my skin
Like a film covering the eyes
Or maybe
A new set of glasses from which to see by
Hopefully a better sight than the last
Is this what growth feels like?
To wander and not get lost
What a rush.

The Fairy Walk

As I walked through the forest,
I saw a fountain.
It grew right from the ground
without plumbing or stone.
It was still wet from the morning dew.

The simple beauty it held
made me stop in my track.
How could I get over such a sight
of purple and green?
Such a fragrance of a summer garden.

I am tempted to pluck it
and carry it with me.
But I want others to admire its beauty,
and it would just wither in my company.

I guess all things must come to an end.
Though if I had my way,
I'd keep this flower in bloom,
until no one was left to spy it
on their way.

Correspondence

I dream of you in the night,
When I have no one else to comfort me.
You're brave,
And you're strong.
And you can recognize when you're wrong.

You fight your monsters and win.
When you dress for war,
Your enemies scatter.
But you know when to sheath your sword.
I admire you for your courage
To live every day,
Moment to moment,
Unafraid of the future,
While leaving regrets in the past.

I hope to see you soon,
Sincerely, your Younger self.

Picking Fruit in Overalls

5

bare toes in the mud
picking fruit in overalls
discovering a new song with every step
singing along when locating the words

You'd call the scene
'Tranquility'.
Without asking her what she thought,
You'd name it.

hair flying in the wind
brushing aside spiders as she picked
swaying to her melody
paint and ink stain her hands

Yes, tranquility suits the image,
But the mind?
Only she can tell.
And sometimes not even she can say.

Summer

There's something about summer
that lifts the spirits and nourishes the soul.
Maybe it's the warmth—
the sun—
or the cloudless sky.
Maybe it's the taste of new beginnings on the
horizon.

Maybe when we put away the sweaters that kept
us warm.
We can set aside the cold
that had taken root in our bones.
The cold will come again.
For now,
Let the summer sun shine.

The Swing

There's a wind in my hair
and a weightless spirit has replaced my soul
I won't get anywhere in this back and forth
motion
than again
I wasn't trying to go anywhere
my barefooted legs dangle over the seat
my toes barely brushing the dirt
this rubber chain I grip
is the only thing keeping me from the ground
and yet
I tilt my head back
and the world spins upside down
or maybe I'm the one upside down
when my butt leaves the seat
I am alive in that moment
then I fall
when I leave my seat
I look down and see the tracks my feet have
made in the dirt
My pendulum path had made an impression
there are blisters on my hands
but a lighter heart beats in my chest.

Dance of the Fireflies

They danced around the fire like wild hooligans
under the star lit sky.
They weren't waiting for their next adventure to
commence,
No, they were experiencing the current one fully.
The trees swayed to the wind's melody.
The frogs sang along in time.

The stars looked on this merry party,
As the group turned from their dance to catch
the fireflies.
They made sure not to harm these creatures or
hold them captive for too long.
They enjoyed the chase and the twinkling light
the bugs gave,
But they understood what captivity does to the
spirit.
They wouldn't want that for any living thing.

It was a clear night,
The moon came out to watch over his domain.
He had never envied the sun,
For he knew the night watch had all the fun.
This was where the magic of the night seeped
into the pours of every living thing.

The sun helped as it painted the sky with its
passing,
The stars gave their twinkled touch,
As the humans realized their dreams under their
light.
But the moon,
He was the real protector of the night.
He supervised the magic.
And when it got out of control,
He was there to reel it back into its place
Until the sun rose again.

This group of living beings knew the magic of
the night.
They reveled in its glory.
Cherished the romance,
And dreamed in its wake.
They even found ways to bring the magic to the
light.
This was quite a feat.
Not many knew how to perform such things.
But, if the moon was in a rebellious mood,
You can get him to reveal such secrets.
Secrets you'd never know if you just accepted
life the way it's portrayed by society.
Secrets you must look for in the dark places.
Secrets that can only be found by the
interpretation of the fireflies dance.

In the Night

In the night,
My hope lives on.

For when the morning comes,
The sun will shine ever brighter.

Even if the day,
Is overcast.

It will still be brighter,
Than the night.

Until the Morrow Comes

A flower in my hair,
Mud between my toes,
A song on my tongue.
All is at peace;
Until the morrow comes.

I will dance under the stars,
In tune with the fireflies.
Until the morrow comes,
I will enjoy today.

Fall

The leaves make the forest,
Without them,
What once was a forest,
Would become a graveyard.
Or as some call it—
Fall.
The forest will bloom anew.
Spring will come again.

Glasses in the Dirt

I like to take my glasses off,
To view the world in a blur.
When the thoughts inside my head,
Get all cloudy.
When they once were;
Lines of precision,
Lines of black and white.

When they start to turn to gray
I lose all my might,
And my grip on reality.
My world starts turning blue,
And I'm not sure what to do.

I'll set my glasses down,
In the weeds and dirt.
I'll feel my face start to frown,
as I try to satiate;
my need for the black and white.
As I contemplate,
My ever looming fate
That's hidden just out of sight.

Living Ghosts

Who are we,
But ghosts haunting living bodies,
Just waiting to be set free.

That must be what our souls feel like,
As they watch our lives go by,
Through their window in the eye.

They sit in their cells,
With dreams of escape,
Where they, for a brief time,
Were let out to play.

They can do nothing as they sit,
But pretend to be one with the body they haunt:
They rise and fall,
But never take in any air.
Sway to the music,
But never hearing what is played.
Smiling when acceptable.
Only speaking the tongue of the age.

Do you pity the ghosts,
As I do?

Are you asking how they might be set free from
their agony?

The sad truth:
They can only be freed when the host is
destroyed.

But that could take years,
Decades even.
And when the body perishes,
Will the soul live on?

How can it,
When it was never set free,
To wreak havoc on the physical world?

So tell me,
Will your ghost live on?
Or will it die with you?

No Man's Land

My mind is a battleground.
I hear the cannons when I wake.
And taste the blood and sweat on my tongue.
There's smoke in the air.
And the endless presence of danger on the
horizon.
They've dug their trenches deep.
In the mud, they sit.
Neither side giving an inch.
They watch as the ghost of what once was
haunts the space in between.
No man's land.
The Christmas of 1914 has come and gone.
Bringing rest to the troops for a time.
Then just as quickly ripping it away.
The new year brought a shortage of food.
And the cold was relentless.
After a time, supplies stopped showing up.
The only surplus was the beds no one could fill.
Their cause had been forgotten and replaced by
another.
Or, deemed unworthy of further support.
But they fight on, not having the peace of mind
to stop.
Will any survive the war?

Or will the hollow men build a ghost town on
the smoldering remains?

17

The Gray Area

As I took my morning stroll through the woods.
I encountered a tree.
Crazy, I know.

This tree was a sight to see.
Not because it was made of wood,
Or because it was a tree in the middle of the
forest.
No, it was a sight because of where it stood.

It grew on the precipice of light and darkness.
I stopped and I watched.
As the sun came up.

Would it illuminate the whole trunk,
Or just one side?
The sunrise disproved my hypothesis.
And only shown on one side.
However, the light showed what the darkness
could not.

I saw now,
That the bark was made of, not one color,
But every one.

There was a deep purple and a bright orange
A dark blue and a fiery red.
But in the center,
Where the light and dark hues met,
That is where they blended together,
To form something magnificent.

It had every color and shade.
But instead of clashing with each other,
They looked complete.

I learned then,
That we must live life in the gray area,
In between the light and dark,
The good and bad.

We must not continue this zigzag journey from
one side to another,
But instead,
Plot a course straight through the middle.

Not in the gray area,
Where right and wrong are indistinguishable
But where we realize,
That we must live with both.

We will strive to do what is right.
And when we fall,
Not if, but when.

We dust ourselves off
And get right back up.

That is where we live life complete.
In the gray,
We see all the colors and shades,
And know we are whole.

Winter

I get it now—
The hard earth,
The pedals on the floor,
Shriveled stalks and dead leaves.

The winter months aren't beautiful,
Not where I come from.
There are no snow-covered fields with glittering
coats,
No frozen ponds,
Or fur-covered sleighs.
Just the dried grass,
And bare trees in view.

But I get it now—
Winter is a time for rest.
Recovery isn't picture perfect.
It's dead leaves and bare branches.

Don't shy from the winter,
Because you don't like the view.
It always comes in its season—
Always marks what's due.
Embrace the shriveled stalks and empty
flowerbeds,
They will grow anew.

Bounderies

You are the reason
for these walls.
You built them;
brick by brick.
You hired the
trained guards.
Interviewed them
yourself.
Trained them to
protect me from;
betrayers,
liars,
men like you.
There may be
roses
covering these walls
But they keep out love
just the same.
You really should
be proud of your
handiwork.
It's a fortress.
No one can
penetrate.
Not even me

No one in,
No one out.
Not even me.
Cause you've
closed the door
And thrown away
the key.

Correspondence pt. 2

I remember you fondly.
So timid yet never losing your hope.
You had a sword,
But no knowledge of how to wield it.
You had courage and strength.
But without testing,
They went unnoticed.

I'm not sure when you left me.
And I was all that remained,
Take comfort in knowing
You have everything you need.
To fight your battles.
So go to war.

Love,
Your future self.

i am a seed

i am a seed
ever changing and growing
i hope i become something beautiful

i am a tree
standing tall and unmovable
i will not fall

i am a leaf leaving the tree
getting tossed by the winds of life
never landing long enough to rest

i am the axe
cutting down the height and courage of others
for new creation or decomposition
i know not

i am the dirt
giving life to all
yet being seen as less than

i am human
there is beauty in my faults
and faults in my beauty

i am life

On These Steps

On these steps
Many a thought was had
Many a dream was realized
Many a worry consoled
On these steps
Many a truth was spoken
Many a question asked
Many a doubt grown
On these steps
Many a well was filled
Many a line broken

More of myself discovered
More yet to learn
The epiphanies I take with me
They will carry me toward
My next set of steps
I'll leave behind the worries and doubts
No use carrying the extra baggage
And look toward something new
I'm not sure what I'll find
But I'll take one step forward
And see what I can do

So Wander On

I stepped on a train to see where I'd land.
My ticket—one way.
On my journey,
The world was a blur,
I saw hills like white elephants,
And something akin to true friendship.

When I stepped off that train,
I entered a battlefield.
My head swam with stories of war,
Yet my shoulders had no memory
Of the weight of armor.
My ears unacquainted with the sounds of cannon
fire.

This quickly changed,
As I was assaulted
By the smell of sweat and compromise.
As I learned all too well,
The price for peace.

I left that battle,
Sword in hand,
To make my long journey home.
On that lonely road,

As I was trying to explore who I had become,
My comrades caught up with me.

They weren't afraid of traveling that road with
me.
Weren't afraid of who I would
Decide to be.
On the contrary,
They taught me
I hadn't become a monster,
In my quest for peace.
They taught me
To love well,
Love my enemies—
Love myself.
They taught me,
I could sheath my sword.

When I finally made it home,
And I took a good look in the mirror,
I couldn't recognize the girl that stared back.

This wasn't the same girl
Who left home,
Scared and alone,
To try her hand at something hard.
No, this girl had scars and a sword.
And she carried herself,
Like she was proud of both.

Like she knew who she was,
Like she knew her worth.
Worth that didn't come from the scars,
But from the courage to make them.
Courage that wasn't forged in battle,
No, it was the courage that
Led her to leave comfort behind,
To leave home.

For it is in the wandering of this life—
To journey with no destination—
Do we unearth what we are made of,
What we are truly capable of,
So wander on.